TO...

FROM................................

ONE TRULY IS THE
PROTECTOR OF ONESELF;
WHO ELSE COULD THE
PROTECTOR BE?

Buddha

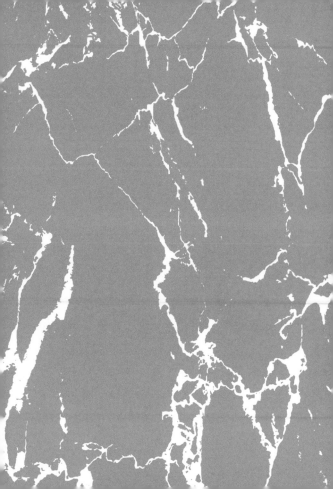

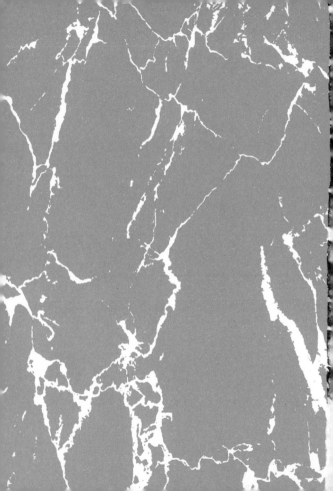

be strong

summersdale

BE STRONG

An Hachette UK Company
www.hachette.co.uk

Summersdale Publishers Ltd
Part of Octopus Publishing Group Limited
Carmelite House
50 Victoria Embankment
LONDON
EC4Y 0DZ
UK

www.summersdale.com

Printed and bound in China

ISBN: 978-1-78783-843-7

Substantial discounts on bulk quantities of Summersdale books are available to corporations, professional associations and other organizations. For details contact general enquiries: telephone: +44 (0) 1243 771107 or email: enquiries@summersdale.com.

ALWAYS REMEMBER, YOU
HAVE WITHIN YOU THE
STRENGTH, THE PATIENCE,
AND THE PASSION TO
REACH FOR THE STARS
TO CHANGE THE WORLD.

Harriet Tubman

IF YOU'RE GOING
TO WALK ON THIN
ICE, YOU MIGHT
AS WELL DANCE.

Karin Gillespie

WHEN YOU REACH THE END
OF YOUR ROPE, TIE A KNOT
IN IT AND HANG ON.

Thomas Jefferson

YOUR VICTORY IS
RIGHT AROUND THE
CORNER. NEVER GIVE UP.

Nicki Minaj

Your self-worth is defined by you. You don't have to depend on someone telling you who you are.

Beyoncé

FORGET WHAT
YOU AREN'T.
LOVE WHAT
YOU ARE.

I ASK
NOT FOR
A LIGHTER
BURDEN,
BUT FOR
BROADER
SHOULDERS.

Yiddish
proverb

TURN YOUR
WOUNDS INTO
WISDOM.

oprah Winfrey

A PROBLEM IS A CHANCE FOR YOU TO DO YOUR BEST.

Duke Ellington

ALTHOUGH THE WORLD
IS FULL OF SUFFERING,
IT IS FULL ALSO OF THE
OVERCOMING OF IT.

Helen Keller

YOUR HARDEST
TIMES OFTEN LEAD
TO THE GREATEST
MOMENTS OF
YOUR LIFE.

Roy T. Bennett

THE
DARKEST
HOUR
HAS ONLY
SIXTY
MINUTES.

Morris
Mandel

IT IS FOOLISH TO TEAR ONE'S HAIR IN GRIEF, AS THOUGH SORROW WOULD BE MADE LESS BY BALDNESS.

Cicero

NO ONE EXCEPT
YOU ALONE CAN
CHANGE YOUR LIFE.

M. K. Soni

INVEST IN YOURSELF.

YOU ARE PRICELESS.

THE WORLD BREAKS
EVERYONE, AND
AFTERWARD, MANY
ARE STRONG AT THE
BROKEN PLACES.

Ernest Hemingway

ANYONE CAN HIDE. FACING
UP TO THINGS, WORKING
THROUGH THEM, THAT'S
WHAT MAKES YOU STRONG.

Sarah Dessen

WE ACQUIRE
THE STRENGTH WE
HAVE OVERCOME.

Ralph Waldo Emerson

A woman is like a tea bag;
you never know how strong
she is until she's in hot water.

Anonymous

IT'S NOT
ALWAYS
NECESSARY
TO BE
STRONG,
BUT TO FEEL
STRONG.

Jon Krakauer

SOMETIMES, CARRYING ON, JUST CARRYING ON, IS THE SUPERHUMAN ACHIEVEMENT.

Albert Camus

SCARED IS WHAT YOU'RE
FEELING... BRAVE IS WHAT
YOU'RE DOING.

Emma Donoghue

THE STRUGGLE
YOU'RE IN TODAY
IS DEVELOPING
THE STRENGTH
YOU NEED FOR
TOMORROW.
DON'T GIVE UP.

Robert Tew

NEVER CONFUSE
A SINGLE DEFEAT
WITH A FINAL
DEFEAT.

F. Scott Fitzgerald

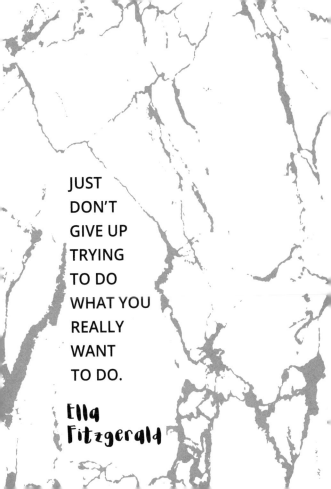

JUST
DON'T
GIVE UP
TRYING
TO DO
WHAT YOU
REALLY
WANT
TO DO.

Ella
Fitzgerald

OUT OF SUFFERING HAVE
EMERGED THE STRONGEST
SOULS; THE MOST MASSIVE
CHARACTERS ARE SEARED
WITH SCARS.

Kahlil Gibran

USE YOUR MISTAKES
AS STEPPING-STONES.

THE STRONGEST
PEOPLE AREN'T
ALWAYS THE
PEOPLE WHO WIN,
BUT THE PEOPLE
WHO DON'T
GIVE UP WHEN
THEY LOSE.

Ashley Hodgeson

TOUGH TIMES NEVER LAST,

BUT TOUGH PEOPLE DO.

Robert H. Schuller

LIFE IS FULL OF HAPPINESS
AND TEARS; BE STRONG
AND HAVE FAITH.

kareena kapoor khan

I'm thankful for my struggle because without it I wouldn't have stumbled across my strength.

Alex Elle

COURAGE IS
NOT HAVING
THE STRENGTH TO
GO ON. IT IS GOING
ON WHEN YOU DON'T
HAVE THE STRENGTH.

Theodore
Roosevelt

YOU NEVER KNOW
HOW STRONG YOU
ARE UNTIL BEING
STRONG IS THE
ONLY CHOICE
YOU HAVE.

Bob Marley

POUR YOURSELF A DRINK, PUT ON SOME LIPSTICK AND PULL YOURSELF TOGETHER.

Elizabeth Taylor

STRENGTH DOESN'T
COME FROM WHAT
YOU CAN DO.
IT COMES FROM
OVERCOMING
THE THINGS YOU
ONCE THOUGHT
YOU COULDN'T.

Rikki Rogers

YOU CAN BE
THE HERO OF YOUR
OWN STORY.

OWNING YOUR
STORY IS THE
BRAVEST THING
YOU WILL EVER DO.

Brené Brown

YOU
CAN'T WIN
THEM ALL
– BUT YOU
CAN TRY.

Babe
Didrikson
Zaharias

Forgiveness is a
virtue of the brave.

Indira Gandhi

A WOMAN WITH A VOICE
IS BY DEFINITION A STRONG
WOMAN. BUT THE SEARCH
TO FIND THAT VOICE CAN
BE REMARKABLY
DIFFICULT.

Melinda Gates

NEVER GIVE UP, FOR THAT IS
JUST THE PLACE AND TIME
THAT THE TIDE WILL TURN.

Harriet Beecher Stowe

YOU ONLY GET ONE
CHANCE AT LIFE
AND YOU HAVE TO
GRAB IT BOLDLY.

Bear Grylls

THE WAY I SEE IT, IF
YOU WANT THE RAINBOW,
YOU GOTTA PUT UP WITH
THE RAIN.

Dolly Parton

FAILURE IS
ANOTHER
STEPPING
STONE TO
GREATNESS.

oprah Winfrey

BE GENTLE AND
KIND TO YOURSELF.

WHENEVER YOU FALL,
PICK SOMETHING UP.

Oswald Avery

LIGHTEN UP ON
YOURSELF. NO
ONE IS PERFECT.
GENTLY ACCEPT
YOUR HUMANNESS.

Deborah Day

DON'T FORGET TO LOVE YOURSELF.

Søren Kierkegaard

BE HAPPY.
IT'S ONE
WAY OF
BEING
WISE.

Colette

NEVER REGRET
SOMETHING THAT ONCE
MADE YOU SMILE.

Amber Deckers

ONE MAY
WALK OVER
THE HIGHEST
MOUNTAIN ONE
STEP AT A TIME.

John Wanamaker

IF THERE IS NO WIND, ROW.

Latin proverb

ALWAYS LAUGH WHEN YOU
CAN. IT IS CHEAP MEDICINE.

Lord Byron

IF YOU'RE GOING
THROUGH HELL,
KEEP GOING.

Winston Churchill

The tests of life are
not meant to break you,
but to make you.

Norman Vincent Peale

IT'S ALWAYS DARKEST

BEFORE THE DAWN.

SOME DAYS THERE
WON'T BE A SONG
IN YOUR HEART.
SING ANYWAY.

Emory Austin

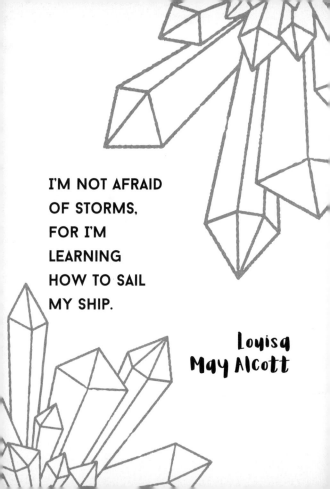

I'M NOT AFRAID
OF STORMS,
FOR I'M
LEARNING
HOW TO SAIL
MY SHIP.

Louisa
May Alcott

NOBODY CAN GO
BACK AND START A
NEW BEGINNING,
BUT ANYONE CAN
START TODAY AND
MAKE A NEW ENDING.

Maria Robinson

LIFE IS A SHIPWRECK BUT
WE MUST NOT FORGET TO
SING IN THE LIFEBOATS.

Voltaire

LAUGHTER IS
A SUNBEAM OF
THE SOUL.

Thomas Mann

BEAUTY IS
WHEN YOU CAN
APPRECIATE
YOURSELF.
WHEN YOU LOVE
YOURSELF, THAT'S
WHEN YOU'RE
MOST BEAUTIFUL.

Zoë Kravitz

Almost everything will work
again if you unplug it for a
few minutes, including you.

Anne Lamott

LOOK FOR THE
BEAUTY IN THE
SMALL THINGS.

STAY TRUE TO YOURSELF.
AN ORIGINAL IS WORTH
MORE THAN A COPY.

Suzy Kassem

TOO MANY PEOPLE
OVERVALUE WHAT
THEY ARE NOT AND
UNDERVALUE WHAT
THEY ARE.

Malcolm S. Forbes

NEVER BEND
YOUR HEAD.
ALWAYS HOLD IT
HIGH. LOOK THE
WORLD STRAIGHT
IN THE FACE.

Helen Keller

YOU HAVE BEEN CRITICIZING
YOURSELF FOR YEARS, AND
IT HASN'T WORKED. TRY
APPROVING OF YOURSELF
AND SEE WHAT HAPPENS.

Louise L. Hay

TO LOVE ONESELF IS
THE BEGINNING OF A
LIFELONG ROMANCE.

oscar wilde

Positive anything is better
than negative nothing.

Elbert Hubbard

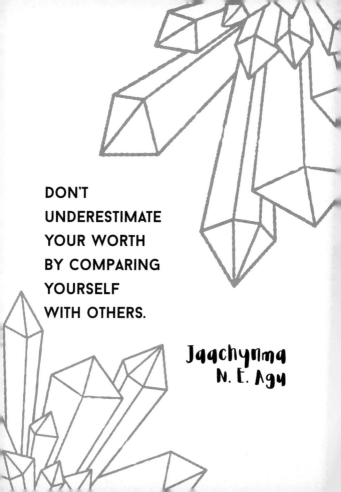

DON'T
UNDERESTIMATE
YOUR WORTH
BY COMPARING
YOURSELF
WITH OTHERS.

Jaachynma
N. E. Agu

HAVE RESPECT FOR
YOURSELF, AND
PATIENCE AND
COMPASSION. WITH
THESE, YOU CAN
HANDLE ANYTHING.

Jack Kornfield

WHAT YOU THINK
OF YOURSELF IS MUCH
MORE IMPORTANT THAN
WHAT OTHER PEOPLE
THINK OF YOU.

Seneca

IF YOU MAKE
FRIENDS WITH
YOURSELF, YOU
WILL NEVER
BE ALONE.

Maxwell Maltz

TO BE BEAUTIFUL
MEANS TO BE
YOURSELF. YOU
DON'T NEED TO
BE ACCEPTED
BY OTHERS. YOU
NEED TO ACCEPT
YOURSELF.

Thich Nhat Hanh

I WILL
ALWAYS
FIND A
WAY AND
A WAY WILL
ALWAYS
FIND ME.

Charles
F. Glassman

IGNORE SELF-DOUBT AND
INNER CONFLICT. DWELL ON
POSITIVE THOUGHTS.

Lailah Gifty Akita

LITTLE BY LITTLE,
ONE TRAVELS FAR.

J. R. R. Tolkien

MY LIFE IS
FANTASTIC, NEVER
FINISHED, ALWAYS
UNFOLDING.

Esther Hicks

YOU'RE BRAVER THAN
YOU BELIEVE.

A. A. Milne

YOU REALLY HAVE
TO LOVE YOURSELF TO
GET ANYTHING DONE
IN THIS WORLD.

Lucille Ball

Start where you are,
use what you have,
do what you can.

Arthur Ashe

THE FUTURE IS
FULL OF HOPE.

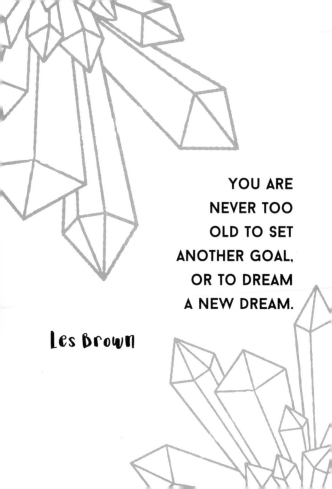

YOU ARE
NEVER TOO
OLD TO SET
ANOTHER GOAL,
OR TO DREAM
A NEW DREAM.

Les Brown

WHEN YOU COME
TO A ROADBLOCK,
TAKE A DETOUR.

Mary Kay Ash

HOWEVER LONG THE NIGHT, THE DAWN WILL BREAK.

African proverb

DO NOT BE
EMBARRASSED BY
YOUR FAILURES.
LEARN FROM THEM
AND START AGAIN.

Richard Branson

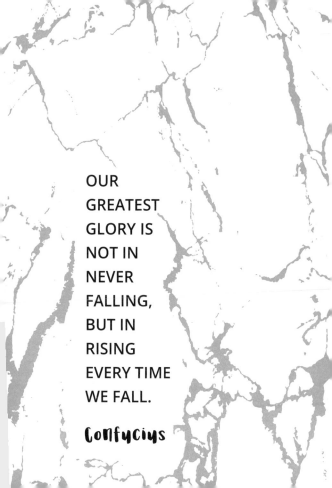

OUR
GREATEST
GLORY IS
NOT IN
NEVER
FALLING,
BUT IN
RISING
EVERY TIME
WE FALL.

Confucius

LOVE YOURSELF
FOR WHO YOU ARE AND
JUST KEEP GOING.

Demi Lovato

ALL OF US SUFFER
DIFFICULTIES IN OUR
LIVES. AND IF YOU SAY
TO YOURSELF "FIND A
WAY," YOU'LL MAKE
IT THROUGH.

Diana Nyad

WHEN YOU MAKE
A MISTAKE, LEARN
FROM IT, PICK
YOURSELF UP
AND MOVE ON.

Dave Pelzer

WE DON'T EVEN KNOW
HOW STRONG WE ARE
UNTIL WE ARE FORCED
TO BRING THAT HIDDEN
STRENGTH FORWARD.

Isabel Allende

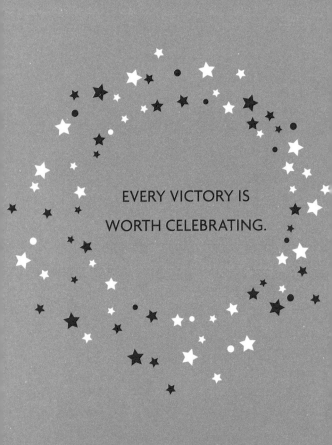

EVERY VICTORY IS
WORTH CELEBRATING.

What lies behind us and
what lies before us are tiny
matters compared to
what lies within us.

Ralph Waldo Emerson

IF WE ARE FACING
IN THE RIGHT
DIRECTION, ALL
WE HAVE TO
DO IS KEEP
ON WALKING.

Buddhist
proverb

MISTAKES...
ARE THE PORTALS
OF DISCOVERY.

James Joyce

THE ROUGHEST
ROAD OFTEN LEADS
TO THE TOP.

Christina Aguilera

IN ORDER TO SUCCEED, WE MUST FIRST BELIEVE THAT WE CAN.

Nikos Kazantzakis

GO CONFIDENTLY
IN THE DIRECTION
OF YOUR DREAMS.
LIVE THE LIFE YOU
HAVE IMAGINED.

Henry David Thoreau

DON'T STOP BECAUSE YOU'RE TIRED. KEEP GOING BECAUSE YOU'RE ALMOST THERE.

Rity Ghatourey

REMEMBER,
A BEND IN THE
ROAD IS NOT THE
END OF THE ROAD.

Helen keller

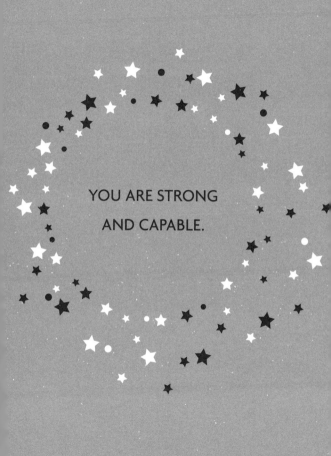

YOU ARE STRONG
AND CAPABLE.

SHE WAS
UNSTOPPABLE,
NOT BECAUSE
SHE DIDN'T HAVE
FAILURES OR
DOUBTS, BUT
BECAUSE SHE
CONTINUED ON
DESPITE THEM.

Beau Taplin

DARE TO BE STRONG AND
COURAGEOUS. THAT IS THE
ROAD. VENTURE ANYTHING.

Sherwood Anderson

STONES IN THE ROAD?
I SAVE EVERY SINGLE ONE,
AND ONE DAY I'LL
BUILD A CASTLE.

Fernando Pessoa

If one window closes,
run to the next window
– or break down a door.

Brooke Shields

FOCUS ON THE JOURNEY, NOT THE DESTINATION. JOY IS FOUND NOT IN FINISHING AN ACTIVITY BUT IN DOING IT.

Greg Anderson

BELIEVE IN YOURSELF AND ALL THAT YOU ARE. KNOW THAT THERE IS SOMETHING INSIDE YOU THAT IS GREATER THAN ANY OBSTACLE.

Christian D. Larson

I HAVE COME TO BELIEVE
THAT CARING FOR MYSELF
IS NOT SELF-INDULGENT.
CARING FOR MYSELF IS AN
ACT OF SURVIVAL.

Audre Lorde

GO WITHIN EVERY
DAY AND FIND THE
INNER STRENGTH
SO THAT THE
WORLD WILL
NOT BLOW YOUR
CANDLE OUT.

Katherine Dunham

FALL SEVEN TIMES, STAND UP EIGHT.

Japanese proverb

WINDING PATHS
LEAD TO THE MOST
INTERESTING PLACES.

IT'S OK TO STOP
DOING AND JUST BE.

Lori Deschene

TENDERNESS AND KINDNESS
ARE NOT SIGNS OF
WEAKNESS AND DESPAIR
BUT MANIFESTATIONS OF
STRENGTH AND RESOLUTION.

Kahlil Gibran

STRENGTH SHOWS,
NOT ONLY IN
THE ABILITY TO
PERSIST, BUT
THE ABILITY TO
START OVER.

F. Scott Fitzgerald

NOTHING CAN DIM
THE LIGHT WHICH SHINES
FROM WITHIN.

Maya Angelou

YOU HAVE TO RELY
ON WHATEVER SPARKS
YOU HAVE INSIDE.

Lisa Kleypas

When you go through
hardships and decide not to
surrender, that is strength.

Arnold Schwarzenegger

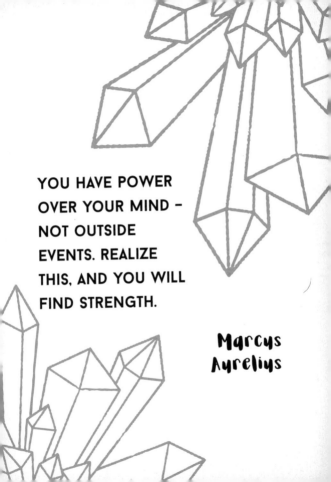

YOU HAVE POWER
OVER YOUR MIND –
NOT OUTSIDE
EVENTS. REALIZE
THIS, AND YOU WILL
FIND STRENGTH.

Marcus
Aurelius

THERE ARE DARK
SHADOWS ON
THE EARTH, BUT
ITS LIGHTS ARE
STRONGER IN
THE CONTRAST.

Charles Dickens

STOP TRYING TO
"FIX" YOURSELF;
YOU'RE NOT
BROKEN! YOU
ARE PERFECTLY
IMPERFECT AND
POWERFUL BEYOND
MEASURE.

Steve Maraboli

IT'S OK TO SAY
"NOT TODAY."

IF YOU HAVE THE
COURAGE TO
BEGIN, YOU HAVE
THE COURAGE
TO SUCCEED.

David Viscott

FORGIVE
YOURSELF
FOR NOT
HAVING THE
FORESIGHT
TO KNOW
WHAT NOW
SEEMS SO
OBVIOUS IN
HINDSIGHT.

Judith
Belmont

TAKE CARE OF YOUR BODY.
IT'S THE ONLY PLACE YOU
HAVE TO LIVE.

Jim Rohn

LET ME TELL YOU THE
SECRET THAT HAS LED
ME TO MY GOAL. MY
STRENGTH LIES SOLELY
IN MY TENACITY.

Louis Pasteur

IT'S NOT
SELFISH TO LOVE
YOURSELF, TAKE
CARE OF YOURSELF
AND TO MAKE
YOUR HAPPINESS
A PRIORITY. IT'S
A NECESSITY.

Mandy Hale

IF YOU DO NOT CARE
FOR YOURSELF, YOU
WILL NOT BE STRONG
ENOUGH TO TAKE CARE
OF ANYTHING IN LIFE.

Leon Brown

You are worth the effort.

Deborah Day

SPENDING TIME
ON YOURSELF
ISN'T SELFISH,
IT'S SENSIBLE.

WHEN YOU
SAY "YES" TO
OTHERS, MAKE
SURE YOU ARE
NOT SAYING
"NO" TO
YOURSELF.

Paulo Coelho

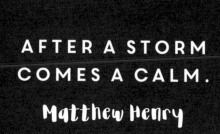

AFTER A STORM
COMES A CALM.

Matthew Henry

RESPECTING WHEREVER
YOU FIND YOURSELF IS
GOOD ENOUGH.

Colin Farrell

I DON'T THINK
OF ALL THE
MISERY, BUT OF
THE BEAUTY THAT
STILL REMAINS.

Anne Frank

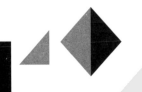

YOU MUST DO THE
THING YOU THINK
YOU CANNOT DO.

Eleanor Roosevelt

NOTHING IS
PERMANENT
IN THIS
WICKED
WORLD, NOT
EVEN OUR
TROUBLES.

Charlie
Chaplin

DO WHAT YOU CAN,
WITH WHAT YOU HAVE,
WHERE YOU ARE.

Theodore Roosevelt

EVER TRIED. EVER
FAILED. NO MATTER.
TRY AGAIN. FAIL
AGAIN. FAIL BETTER.

Samuel Beckett

WE SHOULD STOP
DEFINING EACH
OTHER BY WHAT
WE ARE NOT, AND
START DEFINING
OURSELVES BY
WHO WE ARE.

Emma Watson

SOMETIMES LIFE GETS UGLY

BEFORE IT GETS BEAUTIFUL.

J. Sterling

THERE'S ALWAYS

A WAY.

I don't like to gamble, but if
there's one thing I'm willing
to bet on, it's myself.

Beyoncé

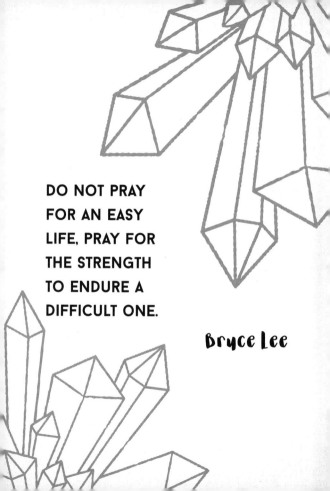

DO NOT PRAY FOR AN EASY LIFE, PRAY FOR THE STRENGTH TO ENDURE A DIFFICULT ONE.

Bryce Lee

IF YOU LEARN
FROM DEFEAT,
YOU HAVEN'T
REALLY LOST.

Zig Ziglar

BE THERE FOR OTHERS,
BUT NEVER LEAVE
YOURSELF BEHIND.

Dodinsky

A POSITIVE
ATTITUDE WILL NOT
SOLVE ALL YOUR
PROBLEMS, BUT IT
WILL ANNOY OTHER
PEOPLE ENOUGH
TO MAKE IT WORTH
THE EFFORT.

Herm Albright

IT DOES NOT
MATTER HOW
SLOWLY YOU GO
AS LONG AS YOU
DO NOT STOP.

Confucius

WHEN YOU KNOW YOURSELF, YOU ARE EMPOWERED. WHEN YOU ACCEPT YOURSELF, YOU ARE INVINCIBLE.

Tina Lifford

FORGIVE YOURSELF FOR
YOUR FAULTS AND YOUR
MISTAKES AND MOVE ON.

Les Brown

IT IS NEVER TOO LATE
TO BE WHAT YOU
MIGHT HAVE BEEN.

Adelaide Anne
Procter

EVERY DAY IN
EVERY WAY I AM
GETTING BETTER
AND BETTER.

Émile Coué

SOMETIMES COURAGE
IS THE QUIET VOICE AT
THE END OF THE DAY
SAYING, "I WILL TRY
AGAIN TOMORROW."

Mary Anne Radmacher

BE STRONG.

If you're interested in finding out more about our books, find us on Facebook at **Summersdale Publishers** and follow us on Twitter at **@Summersdale**.

www.summersdale.com

Image credits

p.1 – 'be strong' © AnnHirna/Shutterstock.com; diamond © mhatzapa/Shutterstock.com

pp.3, 4, 9, 17, 23, 35, 43, 44, 54, 59, 68, 70, 75, 82, 87, 94, 99, 111, 118, 123, 130, 134, 142, 147, 154, 159, 160 © mhatzapa/Shutterstock.com

pp.5, 11, 18, 24, 30, 36, 45, 48, 55, 62, 71, 83, 89, 95, 106, 100, 119, 124, 131, 136, 143, 148, 155 © Art'nLera/Shutterstock.com

pp.10, 12, 19, 25, 31, 37, 40, 49, 60, 63, 69, 77, 88, 98, 101, 107, 113, 117, 125, 127, 135, 137, 146, 149, 158 © Sunshiny/Shutterstock.com

pp.7, 21, 33, 47, 57, 73, 85, 97, 109, 121, 133, 145, 157 © Alenka Karabanova/Shutterstock.com

pp.8, 14, 22, 26, 34, 38, 50, 58, 64, 74, 78, 86, 90, 102, 110, 122, 138 © Valeriya_Dor/Shutterstock.com

pp.16, 29, 42, 53, 67, 81, 93, 105, 129, 141, 153 © detchana wangkheeree/Shutterstock.com

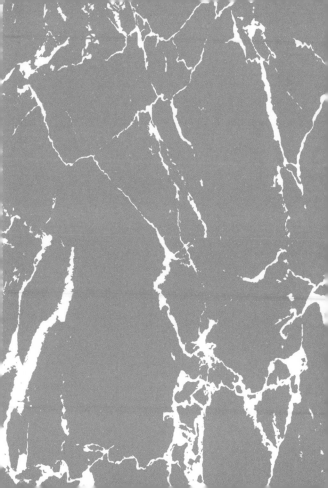

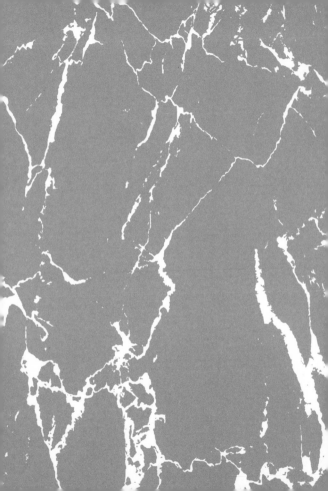